Written by Patrick Potter

A catalogue record for this book is available from the British Library.

First published in Great Britain in 2023
by Carpet Bombing Culture.

An imprint of Pro-actif Communications.

Email: books@carpetbombingculture.co.uk

Written by Patrick Potter

ISBN: 978-1-908211-96-5

CARPET BOMBING CULTURE

www.carpetbombingculture.com

MY KIDS SAY THE FUNNIEST THINGS

Random questions to ask your kids and record their hilarious answers on your phone.

This little pocket book makes the perfect impulse gift for any parent of young children. Toss it in your bag and break it out anywhere. Pick a question and press record.

Ask your kids random questions and film them answering with this super simple step-by-step guide to making fun videos with your children. All you need is this pocket book and a smartphone.

100 carefully selected questions make it easy for you to get your kids talking on camera.

Make a priceless collection of videos of your kids expressing their ideas and views about the world as their young minds develop.

THEY GROW UP SO FAST!

Remember all the cute things they used to say? In the whirlwind of family life, it's all too easy to forget.

What if you had a collection of video clips of your kids talking to camera about all kinds of stuff? A fascinating record of their way of seeing the world when they were small.

Sounds like a lot of work to create? Not anymore

This book makes it super easy and super fun to take advantage of any amount of downtime to capture a priceless record of your kids talking on camera.

IN A CAFE WITH BORED KIDS?

Stuck in a waiting room? On a long journey? Flip open the book, get your smartphone video camera rolling and ask them some questions!

Heck, you can even outsource the project to the kids. Get the bigger one to interview the little ones. Modern problems require modern solutions.

It's going to be all the more satisfying to embarrass them at family gatherings when they grow up.

So get busy now before they're way too cool to join in!

TIPS AND TRICKS:

Here's a few ideas to help you get set up to shoot video with your phone.

You have two main approaches:

- Hold the phone and shoot.
- Hide the phone to make it more natural.

This all depends on whether your kid is camera shy, or just gets too silly when they see the phone is recording.

Make sure the brightest light is behind you, not behind your kid. Be close enough to get good audio. (Modern phone mics are usually pretty good). Smaller rooms are better for sound. If you want to get 'professional' then make a stand out of lego so your phone is totally static while you shoot. Try to center the shot on their eye level.

Make sure your child is focused on you and not on the camera. Most small kids will forget it is there pretty quick.

And the golden rule is: none of this really matters. If in doubt, just shoot.

HOW TO USE THIS BOOK:

FLIP IT OPEN

PRESS RECORD

ASK A QUESTION

THAT'S IT.

You know there is nothing more precious in your entire digital life than videos of your kids when they were smaller. So why not make 'em more often? It's especially heart breaking when you hear them speaking or singing or watch them playing a game. It's a window into a lost world.

We usually only press record for the designated hallmark moments, blowing out the candles, or saying Happy Birthday to grandma. But there is no limit to how creative you can get when you think about it. Getting them talking to the camera is easy when they're too young to be self-conscious. And it's an activity that fits into any time and space of the parenting day.

Imagine having a whole library of short clips of each child talking about their view of the world at every stage of their development. How fascinating will that be?

At every moment of being a parent, it simultaneously feels like this stage will last forever, and it is also passing by too fast. The way they speak at two years old, you blink and suddenly it has gone. And you can barely remember the things they used to say.

Big tech knows this, that's why they randomly stitch together your old videos and serve them up to you as montages. But why let the algorithms have all the fun? Make your own memory montages with dozens of hilarious and heart breaking clips of your own unique small people.

As parents of small children, we're always looking for ways to engage with our kids that are quick, require no planning and will not leave the kitchen looking like a bomb site. Here it is.

Flip it open, press record, ask a question and go!

And, this creative project that you share with your children, will model a more creative way of using digital technology than passively consuming other people's funny videos. Because it's way more fun to be a maker than a consumer.

SO, GO MAKE SOME VIDEOS!

RANDOM QUESTIONS TO ASK YOUR KIDS...

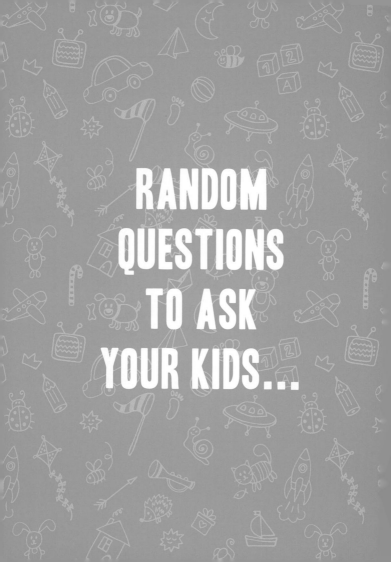

WHAT DO GROWN UPS DO ALL DAY?

When your kids are out of the house, what do they imagine you are doing with all that time?

What do they imagine you are doing when you are working?

What about other grown ups that they know?

What is their vision of adult life when they're not around?

DESCRIBE THE STRANGEST DREAM YOU'VE EVER HAD

Or the most recent dream they can remember.

Or just make something up, which a lot of kids will.

Still fascinating. You could also ask about their daydreams.

IF YOU RULED THE WORLD, WHAT WOULD YOU DO?

(Of course they kinda do rule your world.)

If they get stuck, ask what specific things they might change.

What might they change about rules, food, school, birthdays and other festivals?

Would they try to solve world problems?

Think about the details.

THE PRESIDENT IS COMING OVER, WHAT DO YOU COOK?

Of course you can switch the president for anyone.

Grandma.
Uncle Bob.
The Emperor of the Galaxy.

Ask about the party they would throw, decorations etc.

Get into their vision of a grown up dinner party.

HOW WOULD YOUR FRIENDS DESCRIBE YOU?

This'll work better if you name specific friends.

You could also add a word limit.

How would **X** describe you in three words?

DO YOU HAVE A SUPER POWER?

Ask them if they would like to have one, what would they do if they had it.

Can they do magic?

Have they ever seen real magic?

HOW TIDY IS YOUR BEDROOM RIGHT NOW?

Get them to rate their tidiness level out of ten.

Can they see the floor?

Are any of the clothes actually in the wardrobe?

How likely am I to stand on lego?

Who is to blame for the state of this room?

(Hint: It'll be somebody else.) Tell them this video may be used as evidence.

A RANDOM QUESTION THROWN IN CAN SOMETIMES GET THE MOST INTERESTING RESPONSES.

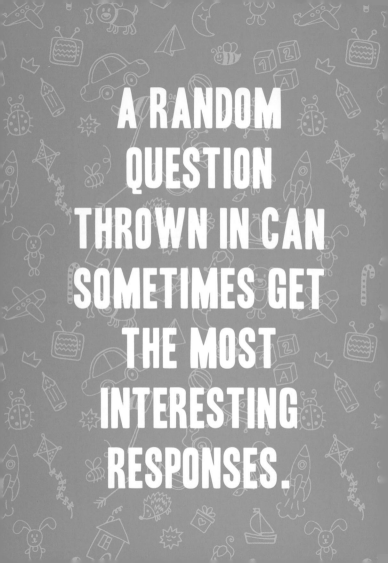

HOW MANY BUTTERFLIES ARE THERE?

You can remix this idea any way you want.

How many ants can you fit on a biscuit?

Is your shadow a part of you?

WHAT IS THE FUNNIEST THING?

Is it poop?

Is it bogeys?

Is it being cheeky to grown ups?

Or is it something completely random?

TELL ME A JOKE...

Nothing better than kid jokes.

If they need help, get them to invent knock knock jokes.

HOW OLD ARE YOUR GROWN UPS?

This is especially hilarious if they don't actually know.

Try, how old is mum, dad, grandma, grandpa? - you pick!

DO YOU REMEMBER BEING A BABY

Many kids say they do, or will simply have fun making up memories from being a baby.

They often have some funny ideas about what babies actually do.

WELCOME TO SCAMP MASTERMIND

It's time to put your mini people in the hot seat. If they can answer all the questions without pausing then they could win a treat. (This 'treat' could be kale, it's your choice.)

Your specialist theme for this session is...

BORING GROWN UP STUFF

1. How much is a carton of milk?
2. Who is the president of the USA?
3. What's your favourite dinner?
4. Who lets you get away with stuff?
5. What is happening in the news right now?
6. Where do you buy bread?

WHAT ARE YOU?

Will they say their name?

Will they say a human, or a person, or a boy or a girl or a secret unicorn or a ninja or a pirate?

You can always follow up with...
'And what is that?'

WHAT QUESTION WOULD YOU LIKE TO ASK ME?

They could hijack the whole process here.

Also cute...

DO YOUR GROWN UPS HAVE ANNOYING HABITS?

You can get more specific than this.

Ask them about what your most annoying habits are.

WHAT MAKES YOU GO YUCK?

Kids enjoy being disgusted.

You know some of the things that make them go yuck.

Throw them into the conversation.

What if I made you eat cold brussels sprouts?

I'VE BEEN TOLD YOU DON'T LIKE CANDY. IS THIS TRUE?

Feign being pretty certain that your kid does not like sweet treats.

Act surprised when they deny it.

What do they really feel about sweets?

TELL ME SOME OF YOUR BEST FACTS

You may need to give them a good example of a fact.

It's impossible to sneeze with your eyes open.

Horses and cows sleep standing up.

It takes fifty licks to eat one scoop of ice cream.

TELL ME SOME WORDS YOU FIND TRICKY TO SAY

Now you already know the words that they have their own special way of saying, so you can make this question more specific.

If you need some ideas get them to say: strawberries, apricots, penguin, squirrel, mayonnaise, spaghetti, balancing, L-M-N-O-P.

You get the idea!

THE ONE WHO SAID THE RHYME DID THE CRIME

You're a little poet but you didn't know it. Welcome to the juvenile wheel of fortune. It's time to put your diminutive ward in the hot seat.

Your specialist theme for this session is...

RHYME TIME

Cool	Cross	Last
Cut	Baby	Right
Why	Treat	Owl
Swish	Face	Boat

CAN YOU DO READING AND WRITING?

Learning to read and write and do numbers is like their whole day job.

So it's a serious business for them.

Ask them about phonics. What can they spell?

Do they know about big letters and little letters?

Are they going to school you on split digraphs?

CAN YOU DRIVE A CAR?

Best to ask this question with a very serious face.

The most ridiculous questions need the most deadpan delivery.

HOW BIG IS SPACE?

Is there anything more adorable than a kid trying to demonstrate massive size with their littlo arms?

HOW MANY DINOSAURS DO YOU KNOW?

This is a very serious matter among three to six year olds.

Hopefully they will also make up some dinosaurs to bulk up their numbers.

IF YOU HAD A TIME MACHINE, WHAT WOULD YOU DO?

You could prompt them to think about different periods of history, especially if you know they're already interested in vikings or princesses.

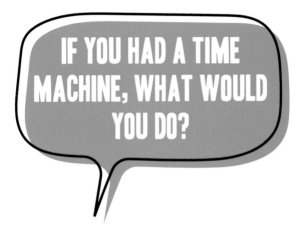

IF YOU COULD TURN INVISIBLE, WHAT WOULD YOU DO?

If they get stuck, get them to think about different situations.

What would they do if they were invisible at school, at the shops, at a birthday party?

DO YOU HAVE ANY NICKNAMES?

You already know all the different nicknames and terms of affection you use, see if they can remember them all.

Also, what names do they have for other people in the family?

Especially any names that they charmingly mispronounce.

I SAY POTATO YOU SAY DADDY

Welcome to **KID QUIZOOLA**.
It's time to put your tiny human in the hot seat.

Your specialist theme for this session is...
WORD ASSOCIATION

Bottom	Cow	Magazine
Smart	Disaster	Coffee
Cat	Face	Heart
Goal	Cute	School
Suggestion	Politics	House

WHAT IS THE WORST DINNER?

Kids are at their most passionate, and most poetic when describing how much they hate the food you just spent the last hour cooking.

WHAT ARE YOU LOOKING FORWARD TO?

Kids live in the moment, so you might need to remind them what's on the horizon.

WHAT MAKES YOU SUPER EXCITED?

You know when they get really, really super excited.

It's usually at the witching hour. Are they even aware of this?

Who knows...

WHEN IS YOUR BEDTIME?

This is a hotly contested issue in most households, and officially the third most asked question when meeting new friends in the schoolyard.

WHAT'S THE BEST THING YOU'VE EVER MADE?

If they get stuck, ask them about their coolest art project at school or kindergarten, or maybe the best thing they ever made with dried pasta, or pipe cleaners, or toilet rolls?

WHAT'S YOUR FAVOURITE BREAKFAST?

Kids love breakfast in directly inverse proportion to how much they hate your dinner.

WHAT DOES THE SCAMP SAY?

What noises do the following animals make? Welcome to the deal or no deal of eternal youth. It's time to put your proto-adults in the hot seat.

Your specialist theme for this session is...

ONOMATOPOEIA

- The cat goes...
- The dog goes...
- The cow goes...
- The duck goes...
- The frog goes...
- The horse goes...
- The mouse goes...
- The ant goes...

HOW DO YOU FEEL ABOUT CANDY?

Nobody ever enjoys anything with the purity and intensity that kids love sugar.

If your kid doesn't love sugar, donate them to medical science immediately.

IF YOU COULD TURN INTO A GROWN UP, WHAT WOULD YOU DO FIRST?

It's the premise of several 1980s blockbuster movies *(that would be immediately cancelled if they were made today)*, so it must be an excellent question...

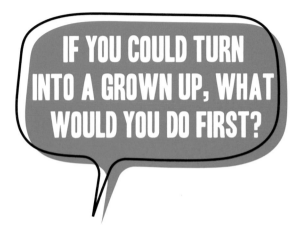

WHAT CAN YOU DO ALL BY YOURSELF?

You spend the first ten years longing to do things all by yourself, and the rest of your life wishing you had the money to pay someone else to do them..

WHAT JOB DO YOU WANT TO DO WHEN YOU ARE A GROWN UP?

This is where you might start to regret letting them watch 'Ryan's World' on kid's YouTube.

WHAT IS YOUR FAVOURITE TV SHOW AND WHY?

We're in a golden age of kid's TV.

Go watch Hey Duggee, or Bluey.

You don't even need kids to enjoy those shows.

Ask your little one which characters they like best and why.

WHAT KIND OF CLOTHES DO YOU LIKE TO WEAR?

Some kids have absolutely no idea what they are wearing.

Some kids will scream the house down if you put the wrong colour socks on for a Tuesday.

Some kids are only happy in a rainbow unicorn onesie.

Where does your kid stand on the matter?

You're a little poet but you didn't know it. Welcome to the juvenile wheel of fortune. It's time to put your diminutive ward in the hot seat.

Your specialist theme for this session is...

RHYME TIME

Most	Blossom	Sea
Day	Snoopy	Kiss
Name	Loop	Glass
Big	Blue	Farmer

TELL ME ABOUT YOUR WHOLE FAMILY

Who are all the important people in their life?

How old are they, where do they live and what do they do?

DO YOU BELIEVE IN...?

Ghosts?

Fairies?

Witches?

Goblins?

Angels?

Magic?

Elf on a Shelf?

SHOW ME SOME OF YOUR ART AND EXPLAIN IT TO ME

This one needs a little preparation.

You could go all out and film them talking to you about an exhibition of their artworks.

Or you could hand them a pen and shoot them drawing something right now.

Draw mummy/daddy/brother/sister/pet /auntie/uncle or even a self portrait.

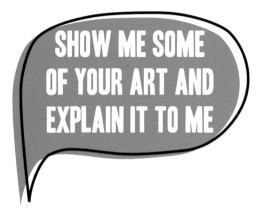

WHAT MAKES YOU FEEL HAPPY?

And ask them 'What does it feel like to be happy?'.

WHAT WOULD YOU DO WITH THREE WISHES?

And if they wish for more wishes they now have to be tickled for three minutes.

DO YOU HAVE ANY PETS?

What pets would you like?

Most kids LOVE talking about animals, pets, their own pets or other people's.

Ask follow up questions, what kind of personality do these pets have?

What funny things do they do?

CAN YOU PLAY ANY MUSICAL INSTRUMENT?

Even better, hand them an instrument right now.

Where is that recorder that you hid on top of the book shelf three minutes after you bought it?

WELCOME TO SCAMP MASTERMIND

It's time to put your mini people in the hot seat. If they can answer all the questions without pausing then they could win a treat. (This 'treat' could be kale, it's your choice.)

Your specialist theme for this session is...

BORING GROWN UP STUFF

1. Tell me one thing that you know about history?
2. What's the longest word you can think of?
3. Say something in French
4. What would your toys say if they could talk?
5. What does an electrician do?

WHAT DO YOU PLAY WITH YOUR FRIENDS?

It's difficult to get them to let you into their imaginary worlds, but they might.

Or maybe they spent the whole day playing Star Wars.

Some things never change.

WHO IS YOUR FAVOURITE GROWN UP AT SCHOOL/KINDERGARTEN?

And find out why.

DO YOU HAVE AN IMAGINARY FRIEND?

Would you like one?

Alternatively, get them to make up a new imaginary friend right now.

Workshop it out with them.

WHAT MAKES YOU SPECIAL?

Hey, not all the questions need to be hilarious.

CAN YOU SHOW ME YOUR DANCE MOVES...

If they're still small enough not to be camera shy, this could be the best video clip you ever make.

CAN YOU REMEMBER WHO YOU WERE BEFORE YOU WERE BORN?

For those of you who believe in past lives, and those of you who don't, this could fall flat or it might be really spooky!

A FEW OF MY FAVOURITE THINGS

Welcome to junior jeopardy. It's time to put your micro primate in the hot seat.

Your specialist theme for this session is...

THINGS THAT MAKE YOU GO YAY!

What is your favourite...

- Thing to do at the weekend
- Toy
- Game
- Song
- Story
- Movie
- TV show
- Cake
- Cookie
- Thing to have on pancakes
- Dinner
- Person at school

WHAT ARE SOME THINGS THAT YOUR GROWN UPS SAY ALL THE TIME?

Imagine living with a giant who tells you what to do all the time. That's their reality.

PULL YOUR BEST FUNNY FACE

This'll work best if you play it as a competition. You show your best funny face and get them to try and top it.

WHAT IS YOUR FAVOURITE SONG?

If they get stuck, ask them what they listen to most.

Ask them what song they can remember all the words to.

Are they small enough to still love the songs with actions from baby club?

DESCRIBE YOUR BEDROOM

Ask them to imagine that you have never seen inside their bedroom before and get them to describe it to you in detail.

WHAT ARE YOUR MOST FAVOURITE THINGS?

Have they got a box of treasures, or things hidden under pillows or marked 'do not touch'.

Do they have a special toy they have to take to bed?

I SAY POTATO YOU SAY DADDY

Welcome to **KID QUIZOOLA**.
It's time to put your tiny human in the hot seat.

Your specialist theme for this session is...

WORD ASSOCIATION

Teacher	Food	Toy
Pie	Smell	Boring
Birthday	Activity	Slow
Potato	Story	Fast
Reading	Game	Mean

WHAT DO YOU KNOW MORE ABOUT THAN ANYONE ELSE?

Does your kid have a favourite topic?

Do they know more dinosaur facts than the management of Jurassic Park?.

YOU ARE A FORTUNE TELLER. MAKE A PREDICTION FOR THE FUTURE...

They could tell their own future, or they could tell you yours.

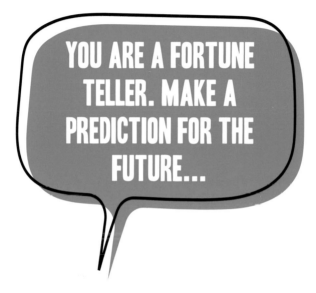

WHO IS YOUR HERO?

Who would you like to be like?

You could make this about role models, or make it about favourite heroes from fiction.

WHAT MAKES YOU ANGRY?

Siblings?

Grown ups?

Rules?

Bee stings?

People breaking their Lego creations?

CAN YOU REMEMBER THE SONGS I USED TO SING TO YOU AS A BABY?

Can you do the actions?

And you will have to sing them.

CAN YOU RAP FOR ME RIGHT NOW?

Of course you are going to have to beatbox for this.

Try challenging them to a rap battle.

A FEW OF MY FAVOURITE THINGS

Welcome to junior jeopardy. It's time to put your micro primate in the hot seat.

Your specialist theme for this session is...

THINGS THAT MAKE YOU GO YAY!

What is your favourite...

- Teacher
- Shop
- Thing to wear
- Thing to do on your birthday
- Art and craft activity
- Board game
- Thing to learn about
- Time of day
- Drink
- Breakfast
- Colour

WHAT IS YOUR FAVOURITE ACTIVITY AT SCHOOL/KINDERGARTEN?

Here's where you find out how often they put the TV on at school/kindergarten.

IF YOU WERE A TEACHER WHAT KIND OF TEACHER WOULD YOU BE?

Mean and bossy or lovely and kind?

What rules would they have?

What kinds of things would they say to their class?

How would they get the class to be good?

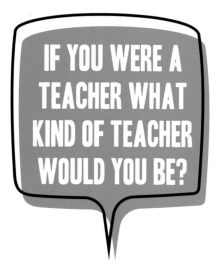

DO YOU ALWAYS TELL THE TRUTH?

Here's the catch.

The answer is always going to be yes.

You could follow up with, did you ever tell a little white lie?

WHAT WOULD YOU DO WITH A HUNDRED BUCKS?

Kids think this is an unimaginably huge sum of money.

TELL ME A FAIRYTALE?

Get them to retell a favourite fairy tale and see how much detail they remember.

TELL ME ABOUT YOUR FAVOURITE TEDDY/BLANKIE?

If they have what psychologists call a 'transitional object', get the details on it.

Where did it come from, how long have they had it, what does it look like, smell like, feel like?

WHAT DOES THE SCAMP SAY?

What noises do the following animals make? Welcome to the deal or no deal of eternal youth. It's time to put your proto-adults in the hot seat.

Your specialist theme for this session is...

ONOMATOPOEIA

- The rooster goes...
- The sheep goes...
- The baby goes...
- The bus goes...
- The train goes...
- The pig goes...
- The monkey goes...
- The fox goes...

IF YOU WERE IN CHARGE OF THE COUNTRY FOR A WHOLE DAY WHAT WOULD YOU DO?

Where would they go, what would they do, what might they change?

Come on, they would probably do a better job than most politicians.

TELL ME A STORY

ONCE UPON A TIME THERE WAS A...

This is their chance to be an amazing story teller.

Let their imaginations run riot!

In the world of scamps, things never end neatly. Even the most magical days generally descend into overtired melodramas. If something is funny once, why not keep saying it for the rest of the week? But never fear, bedtime is only ever a maximum of twelve hours away.

And you can rest easy in the knowledge that you will have the most hilarious video montage to play to all their friends at their 18th birthday parties.

WE HOPE YOU'VE HAD AS MUCH FUN WITH THIS BOOK AS WE DID MAKING IT!

IF YOU LOVE IT, TELL YOUR FRIENDS IF YOU HATE IT, TELL US!

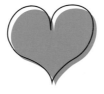

MY KIDS SAY THE FUNNIEST THINGS

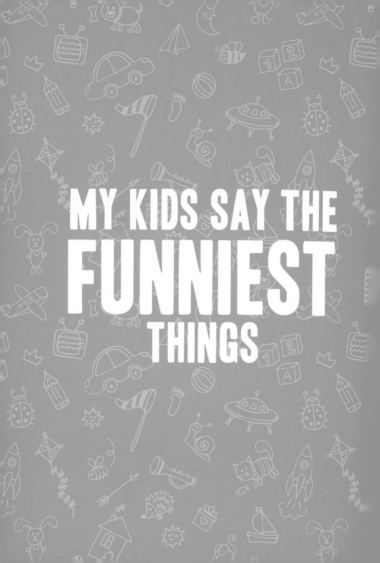